# Family Traditions

# Family Traditions

Gretchen Super
Illustrated by Kees de Kiefte

## Twenty-First Century Books

A Division of Henry Holt and Co., Inc.

Frederick, Maryland

*To my family—the place where I belong*
GS

*To Daphne, Caspar, and Oskar*
KDK

**Library of Congress Cataloging in Publication Data**

Super, Gretchen
Family Traditions
Illustrated by Kees de Kiefte

Includes index and glossary.
Summary: Discusses traditions and the ways in which they are
significant, with an emphasis on family traditions.
1. Family festivals—Juvenile literature.  2. Manners and customs—
Juvenile literature.  [1. Manners and customs.  2. Family life.]
I. Kiefte, Kees de, ill.  II. Title.  III. Series: Super, Gretchen, 1955- ,
Your Family Album.
GT2420.S86    1992    390—dc20    91-45128    CIP    AC
ISBN 0-8050-2218-X

**Published by**

Twenty-First Century Books
A Division of Henry Holt and Co., Inc.
38 South Market Street
Frederick, Maryland 21701

Text Copyright © 1992
Twenty-First Century Books

Illustrations Copyright © 1992
Kees de Kiefte

Printed in Mexico
10 9 8 7 6 5 4 3 2 1

# Table of Contents

# What Is a Tradition?

Every spring, Peter and his dad go to
the first baseball game of the year.
No matter how cold it is, they have a
good time eating hot dogs and
munching peanuts.
They cheer as their team runs
on the field.
Peter punches his mitt and hopes
to catch a foul ball.
"Today's my lucky day," he says.
"My father used to take me to
opening day," Peter's dad says. "It's a
family tradition."

Tasha and her family gather together
to light the candles of the kinara.
The kinara is a candleholder used
during Kwanzaa, a holiday that
celebrates African-American traditions.
The black, red, and green candles
shine brightly.

"What do they mean?" Tasha asks.
"A new family and new traditions,"
her stepmother says. "I will explain it."

"Hit it again!" José's friends shout.
José is trying to break open a *piñata*.
For his birthday, José's mother made a
papier-mâché donkey and filled it with
candy and party favors.
She hung the *piñata* from the ceiling,
and each child hits it with a stick.
"It's one of our birthday traditions,"
José's father says.

Old traditions and new traditions,
holiday traditions and everyday
traditions—there are so many different
kinds of traditions.
There are traditions to celebrate the
beliefs that many people share.
There are traditions to celebrate the
moments that only a family shares.

This is a book about traditions.
A tradition is a special way of doing
things that people share together.
It is a way of doing things that is
passed down from your grandparents
to your parents, and from your
parents to you.

A tradition can be so many things.

It might be a picture on the first day
of school.

Eric's foster mother gathers the children together on the front porch. "You, too, Eric," she says. "We do this every year."

"This is what you get for joining our family," laughs Eric's foster brother.

It might be a summer vacation
at the beach.
Carly and Marie make a check list of
the things they like to do.
"What have we got?" Marie asks.
Carly reads: "Riding the waves, eating
french fries, playing putt-putt golf,
eating more french fries, walking
along the shore . . ."
The list goes on and on.

It might be a good-night kiss.
Rachel's mom ends every day with a
sweet good-night song:

*"Good night,*
*I love you.*
*Sweet dreams*
*Filled with sugar plums.*
*See you in the morning."*

A tradition might be a graduation ceremony, a birthday cake, a way to welcome the new year, or a walk after Sunday dinner.

Take a look at your family's
photo album.
What traditions does your family have?
What traditions does your family share with other people?

# *Why We Have Traditions*

Many times, we take part in traditions
without ever thinking about them.
But have you ever wondered why we
have traditions?
What good are traditions anyway?

Traditions are like a time-out in our
busy lives.
Sometimes we need a time-out from
our everyday problems and worries.
Traditions remind us to pay attention
to more important things.
They are a way of saying, "Let's
remember what really matters."

Traditions give us a chance to notice
the changes in the world around us.
They remind us that nature is
always changing.
They allow us to enjoy the beauty
of nature.

There are traditions to celebrate the
harvest time and the coming of spring.
There are traditions to celebrate the
long, lazy days of summer and
the dark, cold winter nights.

Traditions give us a chance to notice the changes in our own lives.

There are traditions to celebrate the arrival of a new baby and the time when a child becomes an adult.

There are traditions
to congratulate
people on birthdays
and weddings.

There are traditions to
comfort people when
a loved one dies.

19

Traditions give us a chance to share what is most important to us with other people.

Traditions remind us that we are part of a family.
Traditions say, "This is the way our family does things."
They remind us that we are part of the past, too.
Traditions say, "This is the way we have done things for many years."

Traditions let us share our lives with people outside our families.
They remind us that we are part of a community of people.
There are traditions to celebrate being part of a school, a neighborhood, or a country.

And for many people, traditions are a way to share their religious beliefs.

So what good are traditions?

Traditions give us a chance to have fun. They are a way to enjoy our world.

Traditions give us a sense of belonging. They teach us who we are and why we do things in special ways. They make families a special place to be.

Traditions give us comfort during
times of trouble.
They give us peace when our lives are
hurried and hectic.

Most of all, traditions are a way for
us to express our beliefs.
Traditions are the outward sign
of our values.

Have you ever thought about
traditions this way?
What do your traditions say about you
and your family?

# Holiday Traditions

From your town to every town,
holidays are a part of our lives.

Carly's favorite holiday is Halloween.
She loves every part of it—the
pumpkins, and costumes, and candy
(especially the candy!).
"The only problem," Carly says, "is
*too much* candy. Can you believe that?"

Rachel's favorite holiday is Thanksgiving.
When the turkey goes in the oven, the
whole family goes outside to rake leaves.
"Millions and millions of leaves!"
Rachel shouts.

"No, no!" Rachel's dad shouts back as
she jumps into his pile of leaves.

José's favorite holiday is Christmas.
("Next to my birthday," he says.)
He likes to hear his grandmother
describe what Christmas was like
when she was a child.
She describes *las posadas*, the parade of
children going from house to house.

The word "holiday" comes from the
words "holy day."
It means a day set aside for a
religious celebration.
There are many different kinds
of religious holidays.
They are a time for people
to practice their faith.
They are a way for young people to
learn the meaning of their religion.

But other holidays have nothing to do
with religion.
There are holidays to celebrate the
changing seasons.
Some holidays celebrate important
events in a country's history.
Other holidays honor people who have
changed our world.

Think about your favorite holiday.
What do you like so much about it?

Eric's favorite holiday is the
Fourth of July.
His foster family celebrates this
holiday with a back-yard barbecue.

"It's the birthday of America," Eric
explains, "and I like birthdays. I also
like fireworks, the louder the better."

Peter's favorite holiday is called
Teng Chieh, the Feast of Lanterns.
Teng Chieh is part of the Chinese
New Year festival.
"There is a great parade," Peter says,
"with a huge bamboo dragon dancing
through the streets."

Peter holds his ears as the crowd sets
off firecrackers.
"I could do without the firecrackers,"
he admits.

Tasha likes the December holidays.
There is Christmas with her mom.
There's Kwanzaa with her dad
and stepfamily.
"And there's Hanukkah with my best
friend, Amy," Tasha says. "She taught
me all about the Festival of Lights."
They like to play with the *dreydl*.
"And I love potato pancakes!"
Tasha says.

So what makes a holiday tradition
so special?
Is it the holiday foods?
Is it the songs or ceremonies?
Is it the holiday gifts?

José listens to his grandmother speak
about the old ways.
He tries to imagine what it was like to
celebrate Christmas when his parents
were children.
He tries to picture the little village
where his grandmother lived.
"I'm glad to be a part of this family,"
he thinks.

Rachel looks at her family gathered
around the dinner table.
She is happy to be with her aunts and
uncles, her cousins and grandparents.

"I have a lot to be thankful for,"
Rachel says to herself.

What do you think makes a holiday
special?

# 4

## *A Family's Traditions*

Holiday traditions are celebrated by
many people.
Other traditions celebrate changes
within a family.

There is one day that's just for you.
What day could be more important
than your birthday?

On her birthday, Rachel gets to pick
what she wants to eat for breakfast,
lunch, and dinner.
"Lasagna and cucumber salad," she
says. "And a root beer."
"For breakfast?" her mother cries.
"That's not a bad idea," Rachel says,
"but I was thinking about dinner."

Peter celebrates two birthdays every year. "January 15 is my real birthday, the day I was born," he says. "And February 21 is my family birthday, the day I was adopted by my mom and dad."
Peter has a party with his friends on his real birthday and a party with his mom and dad on his family birthday.

"Hey, I'm not getting old twice as fast, am I?" he jokes.

Birthdays are only one kind of
tradition that celebrates the changes
within a family.
There are weddings and anniversaries,
baby showers and graduations.

But not every family tradition is a
big event.
Some traditions are small and quiet.
Some traditions are not even planned.
They just seem to happen.
They are part of the everyday life
of a family.

Everyday traditions are part of the
way a family works together.

For Carly and her mom, doing the
chores on Saturday morning has
become a tradition.
"Some tradition," Carly grumbles.

Everyday traditions are part of the
way a family takes care of each other.

Eric's foster family has "put-up" night.
Each person has to say a nice thing—a
put-up—about someone else.
"It's a weird tradition, but I like it,"
Eric says.

Everyday traditions are part of the
way a family just hangs out together.

Friday night is called "Couch Potato"
night at Rachel's house.
They all sit around, eat popcorn, and
watch a movie on TV.
"This tradition needs a bigger couch,"
laughs Rachel.

Traditions are an important part of
living in a family.
Sometimes, a family needs a time-out.
A family needs a chance to say,
"This is what makes us special."
A family needs a way to say, "This is
what we are all about."

That's what a family's traditions say.
What are your family's traditions?
What is your family all about?

# Changing Traditions

It might seem that a holiday or family
tradition has been around forever.
You can't remember a different way of
doing things.

Some traditions have been around for
a long time.
There are holiday traditions that
started thousands of years ago.
Your family may be doing things the
same way your great-great-great-
grandparents did.

But traditions don't always stay
the same.
When people and families change,
traditions change, too.

Sometimes people just outgrow
a tradition.

Every year, Peter's mom walked with
him to soccer camp on the first day
of practice.

But not this year.

"I'm too old for that," he says.

Sometimes people want a new way to express their beliefs.

Rachel's family used to celebrate Christmas with a mountain of presents. But Rachel's parents felt that this tradition did not express the values of their family.
Now they give the money they would have spent on presents to a charity. This year, they gave money to a hospital for children.
"It was mom and dad's idea," says Rachel. "But it's okay with me, too."

Sometimes a change in the family causes a change in family traditions.

When her parents got divorced, Tasha worried about what she would do on her birthday.

So she started her own traditions.
She spends her birthday morning with
her mom and her birthday afternoon
with her dad and stepmom.

"By the time my birthday evening
comes," Tasha says, "I'm bushed!"

It can be difficult for people when traditions change.
It is not easy to give up old ways of doing things.

But changing a tradition doesn't mean that you have to change your beliefs.
It means that you have found a new way to express what you believe.
You have found a new way to say, "This is what I am all about."

The world you live in is always changing.
You and your family are changing, too.

As you grow older, you will decide to keep some of your family's traditions.
You may decide to change others.

It all depends on who you are.

# 6

## *All Kinds of Traditions*

Old traditions and new traditions, holiday traditions and everyday traditions—there are so many different kinds of traditions.

Have you ever wondered about different people's traditions?
Some traditions may seem strange to you.
But your traditions probably seem strange to other people, too.

Traditions are a way for people to express their beliefs.
It's important to respect the beliefs and traditions of other people.

Traditions make our world a lively
and colorful place.
Imagine what it would be like if
everyone did things the same way.

So enjoy your family's traditions, and
enjoy other people's traditions, too.
Enjoy the old traditions, and enjoy
the new ones, too.
Be sure that traditions are always a
part of your family album.

# Words You Need to Know

There are many different kinds of families. "Your Family Album" will help you understand what a family is and what different families are like. Here are some words you should know:

**adoptive family:** when parents have a child they did not give birth to

**anniversary:** the yearly celebration of a special event

**birthday:** the anniversary of a person's birth

**Christmas:** a holiday celebrated by Christians as the anniversary of the birth of Jesus Christ

**divorce:** when a husband and wife decide to end their marriage

*dreydl*: a spinning top used by children during Hanukkah

**foster family:** when a new set of parents takes care of a child for a while

**Fourth of July:** a holiday that celebrates the independence of the United States of America

**Halloween:** a holiday celebrated by children who wear costumes and go "trick-or-treating"

**Hanukkah:** the "Festival of Lights," a Jewish holiday that celebrates a military victory of the Hebrew people

**holiday:** a day set aside for a special celebration

**kinara:** a candleholder used during Kwanzaa

**Kwanzaa:** a holiday that celebrates African-American traditions

*piñata*: a pâpier-maché toy used as part of holiday celebrations, especially in Latin American countries

*las posadas*: a holiday parade that is part of the Christmas celebration in many Latin American countries

**stepfamily:** when people live together who used to live in different families

**Teng Chieh:** the "Feast of Lanterns," a celebration that is part of the Chinese New Year

**Thanksgiving:** a holiday set aside for giving thanks

**tradition:** a special way of doing things that people share together

# Index